CROSSING THE THIN BLUE LINE

LISA HARPER LERNER

Copyright © 2017 by Lisa Harper Lerner

All rights reserved. First Print 2017. For bulk orders, visit www.blessthebadge.com

No part of this book may be reproduced in any form or by any electronic or mechanical means, including information storage and retrieval systems, without written permission from the author, except for the use of brief quotations in a book review.

Scripture quotations marked MSG are taken from *THE MESSAGE*, copyright © 1993, 1994, 1995, 1996, 2000, 2001, 2002 by Eugene H. Peterson. Used by permission of NavPress. All rights reserved. Represented by Tyndale House Publishers, Inc.

Scripture taken from the New King James Version®. Copyright © 1982 by Thomas Nelson. Used by permission. All rights reserved.

Scripture quotations marked (TLB) are taken from The Living Bible copyright © 1971. Used by permission of Tyndale House Publishers, Inc., Carol Stream, Illinois 60188. All rights reserved.

Scripture quotations marked (NIV) are taken from the Holy Bible, New International Version®, NIV®. Copyright © 1973, 1978, 1984, 2011 by Biblica, Inc.™ Used by permission of Zondervan. All rights reserved worldwide. www.zondervan.com The "NIV" and "New International Version" are trademarks registered in the United States Patent and Trademark Office by Biblica, Inc.™

DEDICATION

I dedicate this book to God, the creator and lover of my soul. To my husband Chuck, my rock, a man that has showed in life what integrity, honor, and respect means. My daughter Holly, the greatest gift in my life. I am so honored to be her Mother; she inspires me every day. My Mother Elaine, the strongest woman I know, my Pearl. My Brother Josh who teaches me the hard things in life, and for that balance, I am grateful. And to my Ruby, a priceless jewel in my life.

For all my brothers and sisters "In Law" and their families. I pray this is an encouragement and edifies you as you do the most difficult job in the world. There are no words to describe how much I honor and respect your courage and strength.

CONTENTS

Foreword   vii

FIRST INFORMATION REPORT

Small Beginnings	3
Never Enough	17
Highway to Hell	35
Intervention	45
Briefing	61

CROSSING THE THIN BLUE LINE

The Call	69
Bless The Badge	83
What I Wish I Knew Then	103
Epilogue	117
About the Author	121

FOREWORD

This book is a compilation of hard-earned wisdom, along with proof of God's love and grace, from an amazing woman that I have the honor and privilege of calling my wife, for the last 28 years. I retired in 2016, after a 30-year career as a Police Officer, the majority of which, was spent as a street Cop (by choice).

During my career, my wife, Lisa, stood by me with unwavering love and support, and I definitely would not have made it to retirement without her.

The life of a Law Enforcement Officer's wife is very challenging on so many levels, which is why Law Enforcement Officer (LEO) marriages have a 75-80% divorce rate. Only through God's help, Lisa and I learned how to not just survive the LEO lifestyle, but to thrive and flourish in it. This is definitely possible for other LEO couples too, and this book will show how it can be done.

Lisa does not just "talk the talk", but she "walks the walk" and she is a gifted, inspirational writer and speaker. I am so very proud of her for finally writing this book, which has been on her heart for many years. In this book, you will see the awesome, life-changing power of God, and you will be encouraged, motivated and blessed, especially if you are a LEO spouse and you take the wisdom from this book and apply it to your life and marriage. Your faith, hope and courage will be inspired to grow in all areas of your life.

There are few books that can actually bless you and change your life-this book is definitely one of them.

Chuck Lerner

Ordained Minister

Retired Police Officer

FIRST INFORMATION REPORT

SMALL BEGINNINGS

*"My Frame was not hidden
from you when I was made
in the secret place. When I
was woven together in the
depths of the earth, your
eyes saw my unformed
body. All the days ordained
for me were written in your
book before one of them
came to be."*

— PSALM 139:15,16 NIV

To understand who and what I am today you need the history. So, I have started this journey by providing the first information to tell you about my life. The story applies to the present time. The power is in the evidence. Time seems so slow when you are young. I always wanted to grow up and be on my own, have a job, and my own house. Now I look back, and it was only yesterday when I sat on my Dad's lap or covered him with my favorite blanket when he took his treasured naps on the couch. When you are young, you never imagine you will not have your parents forever. I was the youngest of three children born to Reece Curtis and Calais Elaine Harper. My parent's named my older brother after my father, but we called him Spanky. You assume correctly if you think he got the name from the Little Rascals.

My sister was named after my father's mother, Nena. I was apparently named after Lisa Marie Presley, but we won't go into my Elvis years. My paternal Grandparents were James (Big Jim) and Nena Harper. My Grandmother "Nana" worked at a Baptist church in Germantown, Tennessee for many years and always took us kids to church. My Mother had all three of us kids before she was 19-years-old, but you wouldn't find any cleaner or well-mannered kids anywhere! We were all baptized, and I still have the white zippered Bible my Nana gave me to this day that she wrote: "Proverbs 3:5,6" inside. That guiding verse has been a foundational truth that has kept me in many dark valleys. We were a typical 1960s family with one of the youngest and most attractive Moms in town. We used to kid my Mom that she was the inspiration for the song "Harper Valley PTA" just to get her riled up. My mother married very young and told me the stories of how she worked at a movie theatre in town at 19-years-old with three children all under six. I would be in a playpen, and my sister and brother would play quietly next to me while my Mom worked the ticket window.

No one ever knew there were three kids behind that glass. We three kids could walk single file behind my Mother in a China Shop and not touch a thing or even ask for anything! No pouting fits, or sad faces because we didn't get what we wanted. My brother Spanky was very good to my sister and me; we never fought with one another as young children. Losing him was a tragedy, but that story comes later. My parents fully believed in and instituted spanking our butts. If we got out of line, the belt took care of that, or if it was awful, we got to go outside and pick a "switch" (that's a slim branch or limb of a tree) which they would use to whip our butts. It wasn't child abuse; it was about behavior correction, discipline, authority, and respect. Maybe that is what is missing these days, no respect for authority.

I was a very fearless kid, and I loved to "manage" my neighborhood. Mom tells me of times when we lived in Memphis, Tennessee; I would just go from one group of kids to the other finding out what was going on and just put my two cents in and go off to the next. I remember clearly one summer we went to a huge man-made pool that had a sand bottom and wooden docks in the middle. One end they had a diving board that was at least five stories high. The water there was 20 feet deep. I kept watching bigger kids and adults jump off that thing all day. It was like they just floated in the air forever before they hit the water, it looked wonderful! Of course my Dad knew I was watching it and told me not to even think about it! Yet, I couldn't resist. I really just wanted to see what it was like so high up. I made my way over in the water and got out on the side of the diving boards which was opposite where my parents were. I ran over to the ladder and just started climbing, no one seemed to be around so I thought I could get up there and take a peek and be down before anyone even knew.

The view from the top was just beautiful! I could see trees and hills and houses and it seemed I could see all the way out of the state of Tennessee! I looked down and decided that jumping might not be such a great idea after all and I turned around to head back down. I was surprised to find a group of teenage boys waiting at the top of the ladder. I explained that I needed to get down and they all just looked at one another and laughed. "The only way down little girl is off the end of that board". One of them was shaking his head at me and said "she is never gonna do that! Girls are too scared to jump from here she won't do it". Well as has been my bent from as long as I can remember.

A dare would be met head-on, and I wasn't afraid of nothing or nobody. I turned back around and walked out to the end of the board, and as I reached the end, I began to hear my Dad's voice from very far away screaming my name and threatening severe bodily harm if I jumped off that board. What else could I do? My back was against the wall and I had to prove those stupid boys wrong and I jumped for all I was worth.

Now to say that it was the coolest thing I ever did would not even be close to the truth. I floated alright, I wondered if I would ever hit the water and when I did, oh. I hit hard, and it stung my legs and butt like I just got hit with a three-inch whip in the hand of my mother who was an expert in the art of switch whipping! Then I had to gather myself and swim to the top. The light at the top of the water just seemed to be one arm away as I desperately put one over the other as fast as I could. I knew I was running out of breath and I couldn't believe I wasn't to the top yet!

Just when I thought for sure, I was going to drown and die right here my body shot through the surface of the water with me taking in a deep, ragged breath. God is merciful, and He is faithful, even when we are stupid. My father was angry with me, but I didn't get the whipping I thought was coming. It seemed everyone in the pool had watched that 6-year-old girl jump off a five story high dive with her dad screaming and running to try to prevent the inevitable and I was a hero. All the teenage boys were slapping me on the back, and the adult guys were shaking my dad's hand saying what a brave daughter he had and by the time he got to me he was just shaking his head and laughing and telling me I had to be the craziest child he had ever met. My Dad shared that story many times with friends that came over and he always put me up on his lap and told it in his classical salesman liturgy that could light up a room and keep your undivided attention. That's my Dad. He was a very likable, humorous, good-looking man. I miss him every day.

My Dad was in the Army for six years then met a man named Zig Ziglar who was a salesman. Together they sold a line of cosmetics/skincare then began selling cookware at home dinner parties. My Mother tells me that we would stay at his brother Judge's house and his wife Sarah would babysit us as he worked dinner parties together with my parents. I don't remember those days of course since I was just a baby, but later when I took my Mother to visit that family in Georgia. I heard some great stories, and was honored to meet a very pleasant man and a very powerful, joyful woman that was a powerful influence in my Mother's life. For that I will always be grateful. So you now have a little background to frame the story of how a little southern girl started out believing her life was sweet and safe, headed to great places. I had no idea of how my life was about to change. My father worked hard to provide for us three kids, and we often moved from town to town in order to book more dinner parties to sell cookware.

Georgia was Zig Ziglar's home then and my father's family lived in Memphis, Tennessee. My mother being from Texas was always trying to get him to stay there since she had family there. So, until I was 8 years old, my family moved from Georgia, to Tennessee, back to

Georgia, back to Tennessee, to Arizona, to Texas, back to Tennessee, back to Texas, back to Tennessee, then to Arizona, back to Texas, back to Tennessee, then to California in 1973. My Dad hoped there was more money to be made in California, so we moved to West Covina. I had never been to the beach, so this was awesome for us kids.

We moved into a three-story house with a big built-in pool in the backyard! This was high living for sure and my constant companion, my Basset Hound Bessie, was learning to swim for the first time. I had the bright idea one day that jumping out my 3rd story bedroom into the pool would be cool. But I needed to make sure Bessie could do it too. So, I picked her up and tossed her out the window with me jumping right behind her! Needless to say the splash was so huge that my Mom noticed and came out to see what was going on. Why she had to look up and notice the screen missing off my window, I will never know. Mom always had a sixth sense when it came to us kids. She always knew what was going on, we couldn't get away with crap!

For a while...

My school in West Covina was the greatest school I had ever been to. The teacher gave you a list of assignments in the morning, and when you finished and she checked your work and you could go home! I only went to school about two hours a day! The rest was swimming, skateboarding, and baseball! Since I had so much time on my hands, I would spend time with friends at their house. I had few, but I had one that had an entire girl's playhouse built up in her attic. It looked like a life-size dollhouse complete with furniture. I wasn't into dolls preferring my Matchbox cars to any doll, but I had to admit this was impressive.

I was about seven or already eight-years-old at this time and the little girl I played with always wore dresses. She explained the rule to visiting her Dollhouse in the attic was that you had to wear a dress. I owned them I just never liked to wear them. To enjoy this fantasy land even if it was uncomfortable and stupid, I agreed to wear a skirt and a t-shirt over to play. That was as good as it was going to get. As we climbed the stairs to go to the attic her Dad was sitting in a chair at the bottom. He never said much just smiled and stared at me.

As a little girl you can sense evil, you just don't know what to do with it or about it. I must have been there to play five or six times and one Sunday I came to play after church and her Dad was standing this time at the stairs instead of sitting. He asked if he could help me up the stairs and I said no thank you. He followed us up and was so close behind me I could feel his breath on my neck. As you come to the top of the stairs, there is a small opening serving as the door to the floor of the attic to get in. As I was waiting for my friend to crawl up, her father began stroking and patting my back telling me what a pretty girl I was.

I was standing there hoping she would hurry up because I was getting very uncomfortable. I remember him touching my back, then my bottom. Then it seemed like his hand wasn't on the outside of my skirt... but underneath. I remember fear made time stand still as those few minutes passed of feeling him touching me in a way that I couldn't understand. I didn't know what to do. Then she was mercifully through the door and I could get away. As I climbed up into the door, I scurried across the floor, and looked at my friend who just stared at me sadly and said "it's ok, you will get used to it". Her father began to climb into the attic.

As soon as he cleared the door I ran for it! My small and innocent mind did not know how to process this. I never went back. The heartbreaking thing to me now as I look back is that I never told a soul. Obviously there is no doubt that man was molesting my friend, she thought that was the way they played. I don't know why I never told my parents. I have thought about that many times since. I spoke to my mother about this recently while we were talking about something that triggered that memory. This event would affect my life in many ways later. The next life-shaping incident in California was the day we went to Long Beach to spend the day swimming. I had never seen so much water in my life. I brought my trustee pool kick board and started paddling out. I kept paddling and looking at the water, and paddling, and paddling. Then I got tired and flipped over and started watching the clouds in the sky.

How awesome it was to float on so much water! Then I sat up to look for my family and the beach looked like it was miles away... I had gone way past the buoys into some really deep water. I panicked and started paddling my way back as fast as I could. As I was paddling a huge shadow passed under me that didn't seem to have edges. I immediately drew my arms and feet out of the water terrified. I didn't know if it was a school of fish, a shark, a whale, or what, but it didn't matter. No one noticed me way out there. No lifeguard whistle, no one calling my name. Just me and fear. The shadow finally faded away, and I slowly began to paddle my way back. It seemed like I would never reach the beach. That event instilled a stronghold of fear in me that would last until I was 44-years-old. We lived in California for only three months, and moved back to El Paso, Texas. I didn't know that this would be the last move we would make as a family.

"My Frame was not hidden from you when I was made in the secret place. When I was woven together in the depths of the earth, your eyes saw my unformed body. All the days

ordained for me were written in your book before one of them came to be." Psalm 139:15,16 NIV

It doesn't sound like God ordained good for me after reading about those events, does it? How could a loving and protective God allow such things to happen? Some questions will only be answered when God and I meet face to face. What I do believe, is that all the traumas and fears that were a part of my life were not wasted. From the things I suffered as a child created thought patterns, responses, and coping skills as an adult I wouldn't trade for anything. Do you?

Take a few minutes now to just think about where you have been, what has happened in your life.

Has it made you stronger? If not why?

If it has, in what area does the strength and resolve learned help you?

NEVER ENOUGH

For the Lord has called you like
a woman forsaken, grieved
in spirit, and heartsore—
even a wife [wooed and
won] in youth, when she is
[later] refused and scorned,
says your God.

— ISAIAH 54:6 NKJV

My father didn't meet us in El Paso as he said, it turns out he went back to Memphis where he thought he could make better money. My Mom told me he would be there soon, but that never happened. When I discovered that my parents were divorcing, I took it so hard my little eight-year-old body broke out in shingles. I loved my Dad, and I could not understand why he did not want to live with us anymore. I have learned through the years from my failures and watching the difficult relationships in those around me that divorce is a choice. Unless you are abused by your spouse, all other reasons to leave one another are founded in selfishness. Hey, I'm looking in the mirror and pointing the finger at myself too, my story has only begun. Don't close the book yet because you may disagree.

We don't consider the lasting effects our decisions as adults will weigh on our children. I don't for a minute believe anyone considers divorce without first considering their children! Divorce happens because we are not getting what we want, and that selfish view hardens our hearts. My parents argued and disagreed about many things. It came down to choosing their wants and needs over the other, in the heat of an argument decided that because of their pride neither would back down. My life took on a whole new direction when my Dad left. I know my parents loved one another, even until my Dad died. It is so tragic to live a lonely and hard life just because of pride. After the divorce, we lived in the Northeast side of El Paso, Texas. My mother worked very hard at three jobs and was not at home much. We no longer attended church as a family and we began to argue and fight with one another which we had not done before. I guess the three of us were dealing with the change in our lives the best way we knew how and it took a toll on all of us. Three kids without supervision spelled trouble, and trouble was certainly what I found.

I became even more of a tomboy than I was before and began to play football in the street with the boys. They didn't wear a shirt, so I thought why should I? Those days didn't last long as you can imagine, I began to develop at an early age and was 12 going on 18. My heart started to search to fill the void of my father and the loss of time and affection from my mother. My eighth-grade year of school I met a boy who was a high school senior. I thought I was so in love, wearing his high school ring until I ran into him and his other girlfriend, at a local fast food hang out after school. My world was shattered. I was so devastated I stayed in my room and just sobbed for days. I began to hang out at night more with my friends, started smoking and drinking, and yearned to find someone to love me. I used to babysit a beautiful little Indian boy down the street. My mom knew this family, and usually, the older boys ended up staying at our house because they would fight all the time with their Dad.

Our house was the "safe house." My mother was a voice of wisdom and acceptance for the kids on the block. Many times we had 3 or 4 kids sleeping over and staying days at our house. My babysitting job ended when the Dad came home one night very drunk, and the mother happened to be out of town with her family. I had unknowingly placed myself in a very dangerous position and was about to pay for it. I was twelve years old at the time and not prepared for the strong physical advances that were made. The more I backed away and tried to tell him I needed to leave, the stronger his grip became on my wrist, and the smaller and weaker I began to feel. My mind kept telling me to run, to kick, to punch him in the face! But my body would not respond! It was as if I was not there I could feel things were happening around me and to me but I couldn't get a sound out. Fear again held a grip on my heart, and I didn't know what to do.

All I could say through the whole ordeal was "No." Once it was mercifully over and the pain stopped he walked out of the room. I began to cry and try to find the rest of my clothes. He came back in the room and put his face an inch from mine and started telling me how he knew I wanted him. The way I dressed, the way I did and said things told him "I was ready." In my young and terrified mind, I began to believe this happened to me because it was what I made him do. He told me if I ever told anyone they would know that I was a "____" and that it would ruin my life. It was better just to forget about it. I never told anyone because I honestly believed it was my fault. This event triggered many responses in my life that were twisted and built on a lie. I began to struggle with feelings of being worthless.

I doubted my ability to make good choices and believed whatever happened to me was due to my actions or words. No one else could be accountable, only me. My freshman year of high school I began a two year relationship with a guy that was 22. My mother was not fond of this guy at all. At 14 years old I found out I was pregnant. My Mother took me to a doctor, and they both explained that I wasn't "pregnant enough" for it to be a child, but it was only "tissue in my body like an appendix". My Mom said it would be the best choice to have an abortion because she certainly was not going to help me raise this child if that's what I was thinking. Fear again gripped my heart, and I didn't know what to do. My Mom was determined that this was the only choice, and I was never to tell the father of this child that I was ever pregnant or see him again. If I did, I would not be allowed to live at home anymore. This decision turned out to be a turning point in my heart and a set up for a very, very, hard road I was soon to begin. No one can convince me that aborting your child has no lasting effect on your mind and your soul. You can't run or hide from the fact that you took the life of your child. How you got pregnant is not the issue, it's the life that began and what you, and you only, decide to do with this life you were given.

When you get to the "Briefing" part of this book I will share a story about this. I began to try to keep my mind from reliving what was going on in my head. I started running miles every day and taking karate classes to help with the anger and low self esteem that was eating me up from the inside. The dojo was refreshing in its discipline and simple order of things. I was beginning to get a little confidence in myself. One of the instructors was a man who much older than I, very confident and had a great sense of humor. In my desperate search for safety and love, It wasn't long until I was at the Dojo more than I was home. This man asked me to marry him and I thought I would finally be loved and cared for. My young and immature mind never grasped the fact that I was only 15 and he was 32, it seemed normal to me. I know, I can hear your gasp from here! In young girl's minds grieving the loss of Dad, this looks like a perfect scenario. Mom never had a problem with it, so we planned to marry. It was a huge Mexican wedding with all of his family standing in as bridesmaids and groomsman. There must have been 16 all together if I remember correctly.

I was to hear many years later that my Dad in Memphis was very upset at this whole affair and was begging my mother to send me to him so I wouldn't marry so young. He refused to attend the wedding, which was why my brother Spanky gave me away. But, Mom married at 14, what was wrong with me doing it? I was so happy that someone loved me enough to marry me and that I would be able to start to live a life away from home. The first few days were really nice. A nice house and I had recently bought a 1969 Camaro that was my pride and joy. I loved keeping the house clean, but I was not a great cook. I attempted to make dinner and was hoping it would turn out edible.

When my new husband came home from work, I had it ready and on the table. He took one bite spit it on the floor, then knocked me out of my chair with a backhand across the face. I laid there a minute on the floor trying to figure out what just happened. Before I could blink a few times, I was being picked up by my shirt which I rolled out of trying to get on my feet. He grabbed me by my arms and shoved me face first into the kitchen wall. He started screaming at me that I was his wife and he deserved a decent meal after working all day. I had better learn to cook or else. He let go, and I just dropped to the floor, everything was just spinning in my head. I sat there for a few minutes and then he came back and sat down next to me on the floor and put his arms around me stroking my hair. I was so afraid to move, or even breathe. He told me how sorry he was for losing his temper and that he would never do it again. He only wanted me to do, what I was supposed to do and then this wouldn't have to happen. My mind was already twisted to accept this… It seemed normal. It was my fault. If I would just do what I was supposed to be doing as a wife then he would not react that way. In abusive relationships, you began to learn quickly that no matter what you do, or how you do it, it will never be good enough to prevent the abuse. When you are in the relationship, you cannot see outside of it. The abuser will consume your life and all of your relationships. It is suffocating and terrifying.

One night I came in from visiting my brother Spanky at work, he was called out to tow a car when I needed to get home, so his co-worker brought me back. I walked in the front door and went to the kitchen to start dinner. My husband had come home at the same time and saw him drop me off. A few minutes after I was back he came storming in the front door in a rage! I never had time to run or hide. In a fit of rage, he somehow thought I was cheating! The blows came so fast and furious that I was knocked against every wall in the room. We ended up in the front entryway, and he threw me against the wall. I hit so hard I slumped to the floor and started to pass out. He walked away saying he was not going to put up with me any longer; I was done.

What happened next is still a fresh memory in my mind even though it was decades ago. As I lay there, I heard a very distinct and audible voice tell me *"run"*! I immediately jumped to my feet and ran out the front door. I didn't know where I was going and I only had half of my shirt left on one shoe, and there was blood all over me. Every house on the street was dark except for one that had a porch light on at the curve of the street. I ran as fast as I could, and dare not look back and pounded on the door. The door opened, and the woman looked at me and took me by the arm into the house. She shut the door quickly and turned off the porch light. I sat down and realized I was shaking uncontrollably. She sat down next to me and just held me without saying a word. She then began to tell me that everything was going to be ok. God had saved my life tonight, and He had a plan for me. She asked if she could pray for me, and all I could do was shake my head yes and try not to pass out.

This would become a "stone of remembrance" later in my life. I never went back to him and filed for an annulment of the marriage since we had not even been married 90 days. Distrust of men stamped my mind, and it was evident to anyone who knew me. I could not stay at my Mom's house at the time she had remarried, and there was no room for me there. I found a small apartment and lived on my own. I was 16 years old. Those were very formative years for me. I apparently became very independent and learned to make it on my own. I didn't trust anyone. My brother was still working at a local towing company and worked with a red-headed guy that just wouldn't leave me alone. This guy was always smiling at me, flirting with me, leaving flowers on my car, sending me notes and cards, and just hung around all the time asking me to go out with him. I consistently said no. After the hell, I just went through I wasn't about to give in quickly again. My best friend Becky talked me into giving him a chance. She said she had never seen a guy work so hard for a date for six months!

I finally agreed and allowed myself to believe that not all guys were the same. I allowed myself to trust again and hope that maybe this time I would get it right. His family would be moving from El Paso to Washington, and since he worked for his Dad, he would be moving too. He asked me to come and that we could live with his parents. I believed that living together was wrong and if you didn't love someone enough to marry them, then you shouldn't live together. I will admit I didn't have many morals during those days but this one. Why? Good question. You would think I could have picked a few more obvious ones, but no. I wouldn't shack up, but everything else was on the table. So moving to Washington with this guy what had to happen? Yep, we had to get married, or I was staying in El Paso, and Mr. Red could just get to trucking. He asked me to marry him. So I sold my beloved Camaro, took three boxes of everything I owned, and we moved to Washington state.

Being a desert rat, I had never been anywhere so green! The streets had moss down the center, and it hung off every fence! My body went into some hibernation mode, and I could not stay awake for two months! I tried so hard to keep myself awake and I couldn't! Finally, my body adjusted, and I went back to normal. The new job there was slow to start, so I began working a few waitress jobs to help out. Not having my car, I walked to all my work which were 1-2 miles one way. I was in the best shape of my life no doubt, but I had no friends, and the only people I knew were my In-Laws.

After nine months my husband came to me and looked very upset. He sat me down and got on his knees in front of me and took both of my hands in his. Here we go... the familiar fear began to grip my heart. He kept shaking his head and trying to talk. I waited, afraid to say anything because my mind was racing with possible scenarios of what was coming. He finally looked at me and said "You are a wonderful woman and an excellent wife. I couldn't ask you for any more. You do everything for me, take good care of me, and yourself." Then he looked at the ground and said "But I just can't do this anymore. I don't want to be married; I want to be free to date other women." Boom. Did you hear that? A bomb exploded in my chest. I found it hard to breathe. I just stared at the floor trying to let what he just said sink in. How could this be? I couldn't think of anything that I had done wrong! He just said I was a good wife.... but that wasn't good enough. The searing pain was overwhelming.

He started talking about all these places he wanted to go, things he wanted to do, and he couldn't do it married and tied down. I excused myself to the bathroom and vomited. I grabbed a towel and sobbed into it until I had no more strength to cry. My head and my heart were numb. I couldn't feel anything; I felt shattered inside. Every time I tried to do right, be right, act right, and talk right it wasn't enough. I almost wished at that time he would have just beat me to the ground. It would have hurt less than what I was feeling right now.

The next day he put me on a Greyhound bus, headed to El Paso. Two weeks later he calls me crying that he made a mistake. He didn't know why he did that and he couldn't live without me and sent me a bus ticket back to Washington. What do you do? I had nothing in El Paso and had put everything I had and was into this relationship. I went back. Sadly, two months later I was on a bus back to El Paso, with one box of belongings to my name. He decided he was right the first time, and his father told me to never come back if his son called again, he did not deserve me. That moment was one bright spot on that dark journey. I was a living shell void of emotion. I finally realized that my desperate attempt at love was a game where the rules kept changing. How can you hope to win if you don't know the rules? I realized that I hadn't been a player, only the played. So if this is it, let's do this thing as long as it lasts. Numb the pain and switch the game. My enemy laid in wait for me at the weakest time of my life with a weapon he thought would finally destroy me.

"For the Lord has called you like a woman forsaken, grieved in spirit, and heartsore—even a wife [wooed and won] in youth, when she is [later] refused and scorned, says your God." Isaiah 54:6 NKJV

Where do you go from there? In this life-changing event, my heart began to harden even more. I was in a state of shock I guess, and all I wanted was to stop the pain. Did God allow this, or was it my choice to trust and marry again? Was I living for God and obeying His word…. no. How do I blame God for a heartbreak that He did not choose for me? If I am not living by His Word or direction how can I hold Him responsible for the outcome of my decision?

"All the days ordained for me were written in your book before one of them came to be." Psalm 139:16 NIV

What do we do with that?

HIGHWAY TO HELL

*"And I say to you, My friends,
do not be afraid of those
who kill the body, and after
that have no more that they
can do. But I will show you
whom you should fear: Fear
Him who, after He has
killed, has power to cast
into hell; yes, I say to you,
fear Him!"*

— LUKE 12:4-5 NKJV

My return to El Paso from the state of Washington was one of my lowest points. I remember getting off the bus in California and sitting on the sidewalk at about 3:00 am. I watched all the drunks walk down the street and others just passed out on the curb. Would this be my life? Maybe it will be easier to just numb me into oblivion and not ever think about the pain. I understood those shells of men that roamed the streets that night, and I felt closer to them than anyone. I knew what men wanted from me, and I knew nothing was free. This little white girl, stacked and racked, was ready to go all in now. Nothing could hurt me now, and if it did, so be it. That's life.

When the bus rolled in my Mother picked me up and took me back to the house. I was allowed to sleep on the couch for a while until I could find my own place. I was 18 yrs old. I began working at a place where the liquor was free for a girl like me. I didn't want to think or feel, just find the party and bring the noise to drown out the deafening silence. A local bar around the corner was a "Biker Bar." I figured they knew how to party and I liked bikes. I used to ride a little XR75 Honda in the desert by my house till I wrecked it and Mom got rid of it.

Probably a wise decision. I was hired on the spot, the drinks were free, and the tips were good. In my new "role" I thought I had everything tightened up. I'm numb Dude, no way in. Foolish little girl playing the big boy's game. I never saw the devil standing behind me, waiting and watching. He was about to take me to a whole new level I never knew existed in a heart, or a soul.

Working at the biker bar helped me earn money to buy a used car. I had made the stupid decision to sell my beloved 1969 Camaro to marry my last husband. A decision I have genuinely regretted this very day. What we women do for love, right? Ridiculous. The next few months were a whirlwind of parties, alcohol, and drugs. I didn't want to think about or feel anything. The pain of rejection was all consuming and whatever I did wouldn't make it go away. I continued my softball passion playing slow pitch for several teams. I tortured my body. However, I could. Denying sleep, food, and drowning it all. I was working on a Friday night when a man came in that looked like Kenny Rogers the country singer and seemed to know most guys there. The air around him seemed to "move" with power, and I noticed most of the guys there treated him with a different level of respect. I was drawn to him for reasons I didn't understand. He was 20 years older than I, and had money to throw around, he, of course, shall remain nameless.

The next day was Saturday, Halloween, and I agreed to go to a party at a bar with a friend. The drugs and the alcohol ran freely that night, and I kept up with the best of them. I remember drinking just as many shots of Tequila as I did beer, which I had lost count. Pour in some hard liquor into the mix and the disaster was about to unfold. The nameless guy I mentioned showed up at this bar and started buying more rounds of drinks for everyone. I was making some deadliest choices that night that would become a spiritual turning point. I don't remember anything after partying at the bar, I don't even remember leaving. The next thing I know I am in the bathtub, and he was leaning over the tub giving me a bath. You can imagine my shock and my dilemma. Here I am, at the mercy of this man I don't really know, nor do I know where I am. I should have been terrified, but strangely I felt a heavy calming that I could not explain. Sounds crazy, doesn't it? The life of drugs and alcohol is stupid, I don't recommend it.

It was now Tuesday night, I had been unconscious for two days. Yes, you would be correct in assuming I should have died from alcohol poisoning. He told me he took care of me and made sure I was ok. He also went to my Mom's house and gathered my few bags of stuff and brought it to his house. The trap was set, and I had already taken the bait. The velvet rope on my neck seemed soft at the time. It felt secure and insanely safe.

I have never discovered all that transpired during those two days. I called my friend that I went to the party with and she said He put me on the back of his bike, she zipped my hands up in his jacket pockets so I wouldn't fall off, and he took me to his house. This man became an obsession that was like a drug. I knew he was not good for me. I had entered the "Biker World" and would belong to him as property, not as a person. My heart was so broken and hard, and my spirit so wounded that I could not deny this man anything. It is the strangest phenomenon I have ever known. I was physically and verbally controlled and abused, but I felt I deserved it, that he was my protector and provider. Whenever the abuse came, it was because I did something to cause it, and it was never his fault. Of course my one moral still remained, God bless my twisted heart. We had to be married because living together was wrong! Really?! You just did all that, and now you stand back with self-made righteousness and say "I won't live with you unless you marry me? Oh, the irony. You gotta love it. What a wretched mess I was. With the alcohol, drugs, and God knows all the rest that was going on at the time, I still wouldn't shack up! What do you do when you cannot leave the man, but you won't shack up? You get married.

It was a "normal" relationship with me. Don't screw up or open your mouth and things are great! He had a bottomless wallet, so he bought cars and bikes and we partied all the time. He bought a bar in town, and I worked it occasionally. Of course, it's challenging to work in a bar and not speak to men who are 98% of the clientele. Talking to men gets you a backhand or a tongue lashing so severe you feel like a whipped animal. My obsession with him and possession by him was so intense that one night he was mad at me, and took me to the porch and told me to sleep there, like a dog. I had better be there in the morning, or there would be consequences.

Yes, I slept on the porch all night by the door, hoping his anger would subside. Why didn't I leave? I could have just walked away, right? Seems easy enough. I can only say the fear is all consuming. Fear of abuse, abandonment, rejection, loneliness, and feeling I had nowhere to go drove me to lay there. That's when you know you're done. There is not another level to sink to, that was as far down mentally, and emotionally I could go. Whatever spark of life left of who I was flickered and gasped for breath. I was dying inside, and I felt no one cared if I did. My choices put me on that porch. As silent tears soaked into the cold concrete, my spirit began to scream for life. If I stayed here with this man, I would die. If not by his hand, or the hand of the world I lived in…. It might be on my own.

During our marriage, I was not allowed to see friends or family hardly at all. I allowed myself to think of what it would be like to be free, to not live in fear. I dared to hope that if I just gathered the courage to run, maybe he wouldn't kill me as promised. Perhaps he will find someone else and move on.

One day he sent me to the store. As I got in the car and drove a feeling rose up to me that this was my chance to run. I wouldn't take anything I had because everything belonged to him. Could I risk calling his bluff? Something in me cried out, and I knew I had to try. Either way, I could die. With him, it was only a matter of time. Risking all to leave, was not. I rolled the dice and never went back. All I started with was the clothes on my back and a diamond ring he had given me. I laid low for a few days, waiting for him to find me. I knew he had been to all my friend's houses and my Mom's house. Through the years we were together, he had threatened to kill my family first, then me if I ever left him.

I took one day at a time, I needed to find transportation, a job, and a place to live. Hoping I would make it that far and then see what came next. A friend from an old job worked at a car dealership and let me trade the ring I kept for a truck. My old job took me back, and I found a small apartment. There was never a day during that time when I didn't walk looking over my shoulder and eat every meal like it was my last.

"And I say to you, My friends, do not be afraid of those who kill the body, and after that have no more that they can do. But I will show you whom you should fear: Fear Him who, after He has killed, has power to cast into hell; yes, I say to you, fear Him!" Luke 12:4-5 NKJV

This relationship was one that a new level of fear. Fear of one that could kill my soul. I loved this man the only way I knew how. Love looked like abuse and neglect to me. It was full of head games and pain. As I look back on these years, I see how God was there, even then. I was not living for God so should I expect His Divine protection? Favor?

The lessons learned and experienced during

this time were priceless and painful. Is there a relationship you have had that has taught you things you can only learn in pain?

Has it helped you later in life, or in another relationship?

INTERVENTION

My beloved spoke and said to me, "Arise, my darling, my beautiful one, come with me. 11 See! The winter is past; the rains are over and gone. Flowers appear on the earth; the season of singing has come, the cooing of doves is heard in our land.

— SONG OF SOLOMON 2:10-12 NIV

My life was about to change in ways that I never would have imagined. I planned to move to Austin Texas and leave El Paso behind. I went to Austin for a job interview, got the job, and came back to pack up and hit the road. I was working at a local Italian restaurant at the time, and that weekend a young police officer came in to eat with his partner. You see, my uncle was a sergeant at the Northeast Police Station. During the last few years of my life, the police were the bad guys. You stayed away and did what you could to keep their eyes off you. My game was that whenever they were around, I would always tell them I was his niece. The last thing I needed was to be seen talking to officers too long with the life I just escaped from.

I knew nameless was still watching me as were his friends. If they thought for a minute I was a snitch, there was no doubt I'd be buried in the desert in a deep unmarked grave. My uncle called me a few days later after these two officers came in to eat that I "introduced" myself too and wanted to know what I did to Chuck Lerner. I wondered, who the heck is Chuck Lerner and why is he talking to you about me? He happened to be the officer at the restaurant the other night. Oh yeah, I remember him, he drank about 20 glasses of tea. I told him to tell Mr. Lerner if he had questions to come to me. Well, the guy showed back up at the restaurant the next day for lunch and asked for my number. Now, I know what you're thinking... Surely she is not going to date a cop? That's a suicide mission. Here I am already waiting for someone to come out of nowhere and snuff me out, and I am going to date a cop??! I still shake my head at the amazing workings of God. I can only say that what I felt deeply when talking to Chuck was a "knowing" that I had never felt before. A deep peace that everything was ok. At this point in my wretched life, I was through with men! I know you can fully understand that after three utterly failed marriages and too many relationships that had sucked all the love, hope, and life I had. All I could manage to do was to survive and breathe. I knew I should move to Austin, start a new life and put all of this hell behind me. Yet, this intense draw to him was so different from any attraction I had felt before.

It wasn't just physical; he was easy on the eyes

for sure. A handsome, tall drink of water that had a presence about him. It wasn't emotional because I knew those were dead. It was a certainty, a peace, a feeling of goodness that I wasn't sure what to do with. Yet I knew what awaited me if I pursued a relationship with a cop, I thought death certainly for me and maybe even for him! Yet, I could not shake off this feeling that everything would be ok that this was right. The battle within me was intense, and I struggled with the thought of causing someone else harms because of my past. It would be a battle I would fight for many more years to come. Your past mistakes and experiences in life is a two-edged sword. It cuts one way to break through barriers and entanglements to keep you moving forward, yet at the same time, that blade cuts you.

Six months later when I came home from work to my apartment and found my ex sitting in my living room.

Everything in my being knew I was going to die. I slowly exhaled and walked to the chair and sat down. I have shared in intimate counseling sessions and with a few groups of women that needed to hear the details of that night. I faced death, and "someone or something" intervened far more powerful than the man in front of me that had held me captive. A tangible presence caused fear I had never seen him before. The look on his face of realizing he did not have the power to take my life was astonishing to me. The scene was a blur, and he was gone. I found myself sobbing on the floor, wondering what just happened. Who or what could cause him to feel enough fear that he would just leave? I had never felt such power and peace at the same time.

Once you have lived on the street, it never leaves you. I didn't realize the change in me was from the outside in, instead of inside out. I made a decision to stay in El Paso and find out what the deal was with this man, a cop, something new and different from anything I had ever known. Making the decision to move forward with this relationship I was always wondering in those early days when I would be taken out. Would I have the lifetime of regret learning that someone had taken Chuck's life because of me? My soul was being driven by something more powerful than I. I was on the road to meeting the one who was stronger than all of this. I just didn't know it yet.

I worked at a local restaurant as an assistant manager on the east side of El Paso while Chuck and I were dating. One of the waitresses and I began a friendship, and I started to share some of my past with her. She told me that I needed to meet her Mom and that God had plans for me. I laughed in her face about the God part. I knew from my early experience with the church that there was no way God wanted anything to do with me now. I had done horrible things and allowed awful things to be done to me. God indeed was just in condemning me, I had already condemned myself. My waitress friend brought her Mom into the restaurant to meet me. She was a very kind person and had a glow about her that actually comforted me. She invited me to her church which I politely declined. I continued to decline every time she came in over the next few months. This woman was very friendly, encouraging, and relentless. One afternoon I had finally reached my limit, but I did not want to hurt her feelings. I finally agreed to go one time, for the love of God, if she promised never to ask me again! She laughed and agreed.

The Sunday night service I agreed to visit started at 6:00 and I had that day off. All day I was very nervous and kept trying to find a reason why I shouldn't go. Everything in me was in turmoil, and I just couldn't handle another rejection. My mind kept telling me all the reasons why God wanted nothing to do with me, and it was stupid for me to even consider going to His house! I was a thief, a liar, an adulteress, even a murderer! There was no way God would even want me to darken the doors of his Holy House. Yet my soul was being drawn to go. As the time arrived to go, I made a deal with God. I said "God I know who I am and I know what I've done. If there is any way, you can forgive me and accept me, I need to know today. If you are willing to do that I need YOU to show up in a way that I know it's you. Not a Preacher or anyone else telling me what they thought God wanted me to know! I need to hear from you! But, if you can't, or aren't willing…. I understand. I don't blame you, and

I'll never bother you again." With all the courage I could muster, I walked in the door of Alive Ministries Church in east El Paso on a warm Sunday night in April 1988.

I sat on the back row of course and closest to the door just in case my nerves failed me. I could quickly bolt, and hopefully, the hand of God couldn't snatch me and throw me into the pit I deserved. It kind of felt like going to the police station to ask directions when your face is on an 8x10 poster on the wall of The Most Wanted! I slid into the seat and waited to find out my fate. If God did not hear me, then my life would really not be worth living, and it wouldn't matter what I from now on. I would never be good enough.

The music they played and the songs they sung were all new to me. I have never heard music like that in church. It was actually good to hear and to watch how people smiled at one another and actually seemed to love each other. Of course, I didn't trust any of it, or any of them. After the music was over the preacher started walking back and forth across the front of the church slowly with his hands in his pockets looking down as he walked. He did this it seemed for quite a while until I felt even more uncomfortable. What was wrong with people?! Then he stopped, looked up, and said "There is someone here today that has laid out a fleece to God. They have asked him to show up today and reveal himself to them and forgive them. God has revealed to me He is here now, and he is inviting this person to come meet Him. He has answered your request by being here, now you must do your part and come down here". I sat there a minute, then looked around, then thought…. for a minute there I thought he was talking about me. Ha! Wait… Was he really talking to me?! I waited a few minutes to see if anyone would go up front. No one moved, and the preacher continued to walk back and forth, slowly and silently. I began to hear people around me praying so quietly I couldn't hear them, but it was if I could feel them.

The preacher stopped walking, looked up and said again "There is someone here today that has laid out a fleece to God. They have asked him to show up here today and reveal himself to them and forgive them. He wants you to know He loves you and He is not angry with you. He will wait here even if it takes all night. We will wait for him."

At that point, a battle within me began to rage. My soul and something else within me started what felt like a tug of war. All of my reasoning and understanding was telling me this was crazy! You are a fool if you get up in front of all of these people and make a spectacle of yourself! God does not love you, how could he?! Yet, something cried for the chance that he just might; maybe I can be free, maybe I can be forgiven, and perhaps I can find what love really is.

My body stood up... it seemed to move on its own! Everything was in slow motion yet my mind was going 100 miles per hour.

I wouldn't dare look up at anyone. I had to do this, after all, I had laid down the gauntlet. I couldn't back down now. I was on that high dive again…. I could hear my heartbeat in my ears, and I began to feel a well of emotion rising within me. I determined that I would not show weakness, or any vulnerability even though that was all I was feeling on the inside. As I walked the 100 miles, it seemed to the altar, I watched one foot go in front of the other. My mind telling me all the logical reasons why I should turn around. Once I knew I was close to the front, I made myself lift my head and put on the best poker face I had. What stood before me was the preacher, with a warm and beautiful smile. "A white boy with an afro" I was saying to myself when I saw him smile and extend his hand.

I took the next step close enough to shake his hand, and a strange and powerful presence descended upon me, and the air around me seemed to stand still. At once I felt a peace I had never experienced. Immediately I was in front of a screen as if I was watching a movie. Scenes of my life began to pop up, and I watched my father leaving, and a man standing beside me holding my hand. I saw myself swimming on my board in California, then a hand pushed my board back to the shore. I watched myself sitting in my room crying like a child, then I saw a man come into my room and sit down next to me and take me on his lap covering me with his arms.

Then I began to see every time in my life where I was afraid, I was in danger, and I was alone... each time He came. Then I heard an audible soothing voice speak to me. His voice was low and soft, yet very strong and powerful. He said to me "Do you see all the times where you thought you were alone? Where your life was in danger? When your heart was broken? I was always with you, I was there to save you from death. I kept you together when you were falling apart. I have even taken your children to be with me, and you will see them again." Then, I opened my eyes. I had been crying but didn't realize it. My eyes began to focus, and I found myself lying on the floor looking up at a ceiling.

I sat up quickly and looked around and jumped to my feet wondering what just happened! I saw the Pastor, and my friend's mother sitting on a front pew just smiling at me. The entire church was empty except for them! Where did all of those people go so fast? There were hundreds of people in this building just a minute ago when I walked to the altar. Was I in a dream? I felt so light, so different, I wasn't sure if what I was seeing and feeling was real, or a dream.

I found my voice and asked the Pastor "what just happened"?! He began to chuckle a little and said: "You just met Jesus." I asked, "where is everybody"? He said "The service ended about half an hour ago. You have been there on the floor for 2 hours." *What?* Hold up, wait a minute. I had just walked to the front, watched an incredible and short video clip of my life and felt like a million bucks but, two hours? The Pastor must have seen the bewilderment on my face. He asked me what happened during that time and I told him everything. I couldn't speak without crying and even chuckling a little... I couldn't explain the joy and easiness I felt. I had never felt this way before.

He explained to me that what I just experienced was what some churches call "slain in the Spirit." He gave me the Bible references* that explained it. Now hold on... I see some eye rolling from some of you right now. Hey, I didn't invent this, nor ask for it, and no one "touched" me. The fact that this happened is enough for me to believe. No way I could have made that up for sure! The Pastor then asked if I would like to receive the Baptism of the Holy Spirit. I said, "The what of who"? He then explained in Acts chapter 2 where the Disciples were told by Jesus to go and wait for "The Power" to ascend upon them. Now this book is not to debate my experience, it is to tell the story. Don't get caught up in theology and doctrines, just hear how God saved a wretch like me.

I knew I wasn't worth saving, He had every right to condemn me. Yet, while I was still a mess, not even knowing how to believe or come to Him... he came to meet me. I told that Pastor I wanted everything God had, don't hold back! He stood up and prayed with me. What I can tell you from experience is this; I felt like my body was on fire, but it didn't hurt. I had what felt like electrical power surging through my body and all I wanted to do was laugh!! Really! It felt so good. I opened my mouth to laugh, and I began to speak another language. Yep.. I just lost a few of you there I know, but I can only talk about the truth.

I discovered later in studying the Bible that this is evidence of the Holy Spirit's activity in you. I am not saying this is a requirement for everyone who follows Jesus. All I know is since this happened to me, I have watched God move in miraculous and powerful ways which cannot be put in a neat little box. God is bigger and more creative than any box man tries to fit Him into. So here I am. Saved, set free, and on fire for Jesus! I am a redeemed drug using, hard liquor drinking, biker chick who is dating a cop. Now here is where things start to get good! Grab a snack and let's get to the rest of the story!

One thing I learned is my faith in Christ is my responsibility. It is mine to share, to live, and to answer for when I meet Jesus face to face. Find Jesus for yourself. Not just church or man's "religion" but search for Him! He created you for a relationship with Him, He loves you right now just as you are. Enough that He put his infinite love and power into a mortal body so

He could sacrifice Himself to pay our debts. Eternal life? You bet, getcha some!

* Revelation 17:3; 21:10 Matthew 28:2-4 Acts 2

"My beloved spoke and said to me, "Arise, my darling, my beautiful one, come with me. See! The winter is past; the rains are over and gone. Flowers appear on the earth; the season of singing has come, the cooing of doves is heard in our land." Song of Solomon 2:10-12 NIV

Have you had an experience with Jesus? Not "church" or religion, I mean the man….. Jesus?

Who do you think He is?

BRIEFING

What a story! Whenever I have shared the testimony of how Jesus saved me and redeemed my life, there is always someone that can bear witness to some part of it. Unfortunately, in most of our churches today we don't want to discuss and share the dark things of our past because of shame, or guilt. Please, don't let the enemy torture you with what God can forgive, and deliver you from. The things kept in the dark retain the power over you and will influence every relationship you have in one way or another. I know there were parts of it that were rough, and I testify that all of it is true. We all know forgiving others was tough, but forgiving myself seemed impossible. How can I ask a Holy God to forgive me for killing my own child? How can I request a loving God to forgive me for breaking all his commandments and disregarding His existence?

There were many sessions of healing and counseling to understand the unconditional love of God. One of my counseling sessions God did something that I will never forget. It is a fresh memory that I have vivid in my mind. When I talk about it, it's just like it happened yesterday. I was having the most trouble believing God could forgive me for my abortions. I couldn't even reach the point of forgiving myself. We began to pray, and I felt so overwhelmed. I sank to the floor and was crying to the point I felt nauseous. As I sat there with my head in my hands, I began to see a set of feet in sandals in front of me. At this point, I wasn't sure if I was really seeing them.

It was like no one else was in the room but me on my knees and a man's sandaled feet in front of me. All of a sudden, I knew who this was, and it tore me apart inside. I knew this had to be Jesus! And He was standing in front of me! He knew and could see all of my guilt, my shame, my horrible acts could not be hidden from Him! I bowed my head lower and wept. Then I opened my eyes and saw I was holding a white sheet in my hands that were covered in blood. I knew immediately it was from my children. He squatted down in front of me and offered both of His hands to take it. I slowly gave it to Him and just shook all over.

Once He had it in His hands, it became pure white, and the blood stains were gone! I sat up a bit and looked forward. He wasn't squatting there in front of me any longer, He was a distance away, and He had children around Him. They were smiling and laughing and holding His hands. My heart melted back into one piece as I looked upon my children. I knew they were mine. He said "I have them, they are here with me. When you come, they will know you, and you will see them". Wow. I know it sounds incredible, and if I had not experienced it, it would seem a bit crazy. All I can say to you is I know my sin has been forgiven, and I can forgive myself since His sacrifice was enough. When it is my turn to die and go home to be with Jesus, my precious children will know me, and I will meet them.

There is not a way to come through these pages and look you in the eye and tell you about the infinite depth of the love of God. If there was, I would do it! I have prayed over this book that those who traveled parts of my road will hear the Holy Spirit who whispers to you now. He is never far from you, and His eyes are always tenderly watching you. Not as a harsh judge but a loving Father. Some may not know what that looks like. I understand. My earthly father abandoned me, he didn't protect me, and he broke my heart. Learning that my Heavenly Father is nothing like my Dad melted the wall of ice that kept me "safe" from pain. I had to get into the Word of God to find out who Jesus was. I heard of Him. I was told stories about Him. But I wanted to know the One that just radically took my pain and gave me joy!

I want to know Him for *me*, not what someone else thinks about Him. I encourage you to discover for yourself who Jesus is. If you draw near to Him, He will draw near to you. No doubt. He says He is no respecter of persons, that if you come to Him and ask for wisdom, He will give it to you! The key to understanding what His Word says is to first believe that He is who He says He is. Faith is the substance of things hoped for, the evidence of things not seen. That's in the New Testament in Hebrews 11:1. What I can assure you of is that I had the "substance." I wanted and hoped for freedom, joy, power, wisdom, and last but not least I wanted to live forever! Don't you?! The truth is that now I have the evidence of all of that! Not sure? Let's read now into what has become of this one life. The rest of the story is fantastic so put your boots on.

CROSSING THE THIN BLUE LINE

THE CALL

For the policeman does not frighten people who are doing right, but those doing evil will always fear him. So if you don't want to be afraid, keep the laws, and you will get along well. The policeman is sent by God to help you. But if you are doing something wrong, of course, you should be afraid, for he will have you punished. He is sent by God for that very purpose.

— ROMANS 13:3-5 TLB

My life had just changed drastically. I was in a relationship with this good-looking cop and had cut all ties with the biker lifestyle and all of its vices. I was ready to tell everyone I met about Jesus. If He could have mercy on someone like me and wipe away all I had ever done, He could and would certainly do it for anyone else!

The issue with being in a "sinful" lifestyle I had to realize life as I knew it would be drastically different. I had to tell Chuck first and let him decide if he wanted to continue a relationship with a Jesus freak or bow out. We had already physically been together so that would mean no more of that till I got married. So, you see my dilemma, I really liked this guy! He readily accepted the challenge and was baptized in a backyard pool. Life was good. I no longer had the fear that used to sit on my shoulder and live in my gut. I knew that my past might someday come to visit, but I no lingered feared it. If I died, I was going home, and no one had the power to take my life unless

God allowed it. Period. Chuck and I married in May 1989.

We planned a wedding with invitations and a big cake since this was Chuck's first marriage. I know, God has been merciful to me and so gracious to bring such a good man to me. I knew I didn't deserve it, but that's what grace is, isn't it? The week of our wedding my only sister, Nena, died at 26 years old. She had a form of epilepsy from a young age and had a seizure and died. It was devastating to my family and I didn't understand the timing. My sister and I were getting closer and this would be the first time she would be my Maid of Honor.

The wedding became just us and our moms, no one could celebrate after such a tragedy. This was to be my first challenge with grief as a Disciple of Christ. In deep pain, you are given a choice. Do you revert back to your old ways and drown your sorrows? Do you pick a fight so you can feel as much pain as you can give? I discovered that Jesus was more than enough. I found that I had hope amidst the deep sorrow. Even the times when I didn't know what to say, how to act, how I was also living. God spoke for me, he led me, and he kept me moving until I could see in the dark to make my way.

Chuck and I bought his Mom's house on the Northeast side of El Paso and started our lives. How could I minister to people and who should I minister too? I spent the first year diving into the Word of God. I wanted to know for myself who he was and what he said. It was fascinating to learn not only history and genealogy but how small insignificant me fit into all of that! I had to learn a new culture, the police life. It was very different from what I thought it would be. I had spent my teenage and young adult life running and hiding from cops. I never saw them as people like me, or men who had families and a life outside of that uniform. As I watched them I knew this was where our ministry would be. They saw so much negative and tragic things, every day they went to work they were a target.

My heart began to break for them and their families. I discovered statistics that said their divorce rate was 75% and the suicide rate was two times the average rate. Wow. What would cause such drastic statistics? I started a bible study at my house about a year after we were married for any police wives who wanted to attend. I began to realize that no matter what race, background, or where they were born these guys were the same! They shared the same outlook, responses, and characteristics. We laughed at each other when one wife would say something about her husband and each one of us would exclaim "mine too!" This was definitely a subculture within our country. It had male/female, every race, every creed, and it was an all-inclusive family only understood by those who lived in it. When I tried to talk about our lives and struggles with my friends who were not police families they couldn't understand. Of course if you had anything negative to say about police, we were done.

I tried many times those first years to explain how these officers willingly chose to go out and keep you and your city safe. They have to defend themselves from the criminal element and take them off the streets so you don't have to deal with them. They miss birthdays, anniversaries, and work all the holidays. They know when they go to work they are the line between you and whatever evil is out there. You can spit in their face one minute and the next minute that same officer would put his life on the line to save you. They don't just protect the good people of society they risk their lives for the bad too. Would you do that? Would you leave your family every day knowing you may not come home? It is a very real possibility that you might die today because of that gun and badge you wear?

I know I couldn't. I could not go to a domestic violence call where a man has beaten his wife to a pulp, threw her baby against the wall, and broke the puppy's neck and remain professional. Could you? My husband answered a call where they said their infant had fallen off the bed. When he got there and inspected the baby, he found that the skull was like Jello. There was no way that baby had fallen. Another call was a motor vehicle accident where a child was sitting on his mother's lap in the front seat and it had gone into the windshield, decapitating the child. What does a person do with these visual and emotional scars that sear their minds and hearts? How do they deal with such trauma day in and day out without it affecting their psyche? How do they stay "normal" Dads and moms, husbands and wives when they work in a war zone? They don't. Yet they all choose to go out every day and do it again, and again. Even when you hate them, when you resent them, they are there to help you.

I remember the time I was working on the westside of town, we lived in the northeast, and I saw the news. There was a barricaded subject that was in his two-story house shooting out his window at Police. Apparently, he was a military soldier upset with his family. Now, this happened to be the one day in Chuck's career that he was working a particular assignment. They worked in plain clothes trying to stop a ring of thieves in a residential area. Of course, he didn't have his bulletproof vest on, and of course, he came to this call! As a wife, watching this unfold on television I knew he was there, and I knew he was in plain clothes with no vest.

What can I do? Pray! I can't go there, or call him, or even call the dispatch. They won't tell me anything, not even if he is on the scene. So, I took a break and prayed. Took a deep breath and got back to work. God and I had already made a deal. He promised me that my husband was in the palm of His hand, and no one could snatch him out of it unless He allowed it. So if this were the day, it would be the day. If it weren't, he would call me when he can.

Crazy life this honorable calling is. Whatever you had told yourself, believe that when he signed up, so did you. The best thing that happened to us was the birth of our daughter in 1991. You know from the first part of this book that I had made some terrible decisions in my young life. I chose to kill my unborn children, and part of me believed I didn't deserve to have children ever. Yet, through God's mercy and grace, we had a perfect little girl. Yes, I will say excellent. She hardly ever fussed, she slept through the night, she put herself to bed! What child does that right? Like I said she is the living example of God restoring what the enemy had stolen, and she has always been a gift to us. She is a beautiful grown woman now. She graduated from Southwestern Assemblies of God University in 2012. Now Mom and Dad are on the hunt for Mr. Right! She is quite a catch, and he who finds her will be a very blessed man!

When our daughter was six months old, Chuck was a Field Training Officer and was training a new rookie. They had just had lunch at the local pizza joint, and Chuck became sick. His partner was driving and noticed Chuck was profusely sweating, soaking his uniform shirt in just a few minutes. He asked his rookie to take him home. Now, why didn't his rookie take him to a hospital? Because when your FTO says to take you home that's what you do. When Chuck walked in the door, his face was so swollen, I couldn't even recognize him! He walked past me down the hall to our bedroom and mumbled something about a shower. I asked his rookie "what happened?!" He told me they had just eaten lunch and all of a sudden, he got sick and wanted to go home. I went back into our bedroom, and he was in the bathroom shower, slumped on the floor.

My mind raced with two thoughts, do I call 911, or do I put him in the car and take him to the hospital? When he wouldn't answer my questions, I asked his partner to get a bus quickly! Before the ambulance arrived, I had been able to get him dried off and put some sweatpants and a t-shirt on him. The EMTs came and started to access him and found no blood pressure. So they stabbed an EpiPen into each thigh and started an IV. They loaded him up and went Code 3 to the nearest hospital. I called a good friend, and she and her husband came to stay with her while I went with him in the ambulance. It was another crossroads of faith. What can I do? Pray!

At the hospital, they determined that he was poisoned. Someone working at the pizza place had put something in his drink that caused him to go into anaphylactic shock. The doctor told me that if I had not called 911 and drove him instead, he probably would have not survived.

Of course, the guy quit the restaurant and wasn't a legal resident of the U.S., so we could never find him. That is something most civilians don't think about. These officers usually have to eat at a local restaurant for their one meal per shift if they even get one. If they see someone they have arrested, they will not eat there. I have heard countless stories of spit in food, roaches on burgers, snot in a snow cone, it is crazy! Yes, people actually put things in officer's food when they come in uniform to eat. That's a fact. Now not everyone, nor every restaurant.

These days we have people refusing to even serve them at all! Hard to keep a packed lunch in the trunk when you have to drive crazy to catch stupid people, and it stays cold enough to eat. Some agencies have a great facility where they can eat there and bring their lunch, but many agencies do not. Also, they run call to call so they have to be ready to jump up and leave at a moment's notice. We know the many, many, times we plan to meet our husbands for lunch and they never make it or they must leave in the middle of it. Right?!

We continued to reach out to our police community until we moved to the Dallas/Fort Worth, Texas area in 1995. Chuck had always planned to retire in El Paso, but each of our extended families moved away. When we arrived in Fort Worth, it was a bit of a shock to see how big this area was! I saw stacked freeways and six lane roads. That was crazy to me! Chuck started working as a Lieutenant for a Dallas County College Police Department right after we got there. Of course, he just came from the streets of El Paso, so walking a campus was like putting a tiger in a cage. He was the first officer to ever arrest anyone on campus. Go figure, I guess you aren't supposed to do real police work in those jobs! Next, he worked for a police department at a local hospital, and he had a great time with a great group of guys there.

I felt so different with him still being in uniform and not working overtime, have a "normal" schedule, and not working the streets. I knew it wouldn't last though. I knew eventually that calling on his life to be a street Cop would come back and would not be denied. In 1999 we moved to Johnson County, and Chuck started work at Cleburne Police Department in Cleburne, Texas. Not too big of a town, and I knew he would be so much happier patrolling again. In 2000 we started implementing a national program "Adopt–A–Cop" in the

Johnson County, Texas area. We signed up officers that were interested and assigned them to church members who committed to pray for them, send birthday cards, and anniversary cards. In 2001, we went to a Pastor's School in Phoenix, Arizona and had a booth there for police ministry. During that trip, we dug into what we knew we were called to do. There had to be more ways we could support and reach out to our Blue Family. On the plane home, we got the name that encompassed our vision and founded Bless The Badge Ministry. A ministry truly for law enforcement, by law enforcement.

"For the policeman does not frighten people who are doing right, but those doing evil will always fear him. So if you don't want to be afraid, keep the laws, and you will get along well. The policeman is sent by God to help you. But if you are doing something wrong, of course, you should be afraid, for he will have you punished. He is sent by God for that very purpose." Romans 13:3-5 (TLB)

BLESS THE BADGE

Blessed are those who hunger and thirst for righteousness, for they will be filled. Blessed are the merciful, for they will be shown mercy. Blessed are the pure in heart, for they will see God. Blessed are the peacemakers, for they will be called children of God.

— MATTHEW 5:6-10
NKJV

We understand that most of us won't open up or have an in-depth conversation with someone who is not law enforcement. If you don't walk their life, you can't speak to it. Please understand, I am in no way saying that anyone who is not in law enforcement, but has the heart for them cannot reach them. It will just take much more time, and presence to do that. You will really have to be invested in them, their families, and their lives to earn the privilege of entering this tight community. To understand this subculture, you have to accept that they primarily live paranoid lives. For a good reason.

What does that look like? They spend their working hours in an environment where they must remain hyper-vigilant for the duration of their shift. If you remember anything from this book, remember this. You need to have in your home at all times, to read and refer back to, the book "Emotional Survival For Law Enforcement" by Dr. Kevin Gilmartin. This guy is legit, he was a Deputy in Arizona for about 30 years then became a psychologist. He knows of what he speaks and when I read that book back in about 2006 it was a definite game changer! What we need to know about hyper-vigilance is how it physiologically affects officers. There are changes chemically that happen in the body and the brain they are not able to change. This book explains how the adrenaline and cortisol released when in a hyper-vigilant state enhances sight, strength, cognitive processing, and all the body's tools used in the "fight or flight" state. Of course, we know officers don't have the flight option. When they are on duty they constantly scan their surroundings for threats. Every minute, of every hour. If they work a twelve-hour shift, then they are in that state for twelve hours at least. Do you know how long it usually takes to fully return to normal? 18-24 hours. Do you know when their next shift is? In twelve hours. So, the cycle basically goes like this: They go on shift, raise their chemicals in their body, and brain to be on high alert, to be an efficient, safe officer. We know that every action as an equal and opposite reaction, right? So, when they get off shift, they will swing extreme low in comparative to the extreme high they had just been on. What does that look like? Well, they probably don't want to make another decision, at all. They will sit in a chair and zone out at the television, or play a video game, or maybe just want to crash and sleep. Those of us who have been home waiting for them, so we can meet them at the door with:

"How was your day"

"What happened today"?

"Did you get any arrests"?

"Here are you kids I have had them all day?" Right?

We love them, we are interested in their jobs, and what is going on for the 80% of their lives we are not there for! How we can help them and ourselves is to give them a time frame to recover a bit. I learned to just meet him at the door with a smile or kiss, give him a glass of tea, and leave him alone. We set a time frame on this though. We had a conversation that went like "I know you need some space when you get home, so let's decide how much time would be good for you before we engage." We agreed on 45 minutes. So, after the 45 minutes doing whatever he chose to do to recover, he then had to engage and be a husband, and father.

Your time might be more or less, the point is to allow them time to refocus and regroup their minds, allow the chemical reactions to simmer a bit, and then engage. This can be so freeing and healing when we as spouses understand that it isn't that they don't want to talk to us! It's not that they are so happy at work then tired, drained, and sometimes unresponsive to us at home because we have done something wrong. No! They are "pumped" at work because they are hyper-vigilant and must be to stay alive! The after effect is the recovery physically and psychologically. This is where extra jobs can be dangerous. Now hear me, I will never judge someone's financial situation and what they decide is best for their family.

All I am saying is that once you understand the hyper-vigilance cycle, you might want to really look at it again. Is it worth the price to have them work on the times they have to recover, and be with family? If it's absolutely necessary, then you don't have a choice. Unless you reevaluate where he works and maybe an agency move might be worth considering. That's a family decision based on the big picture of his health and your life together. If it really isn't imperative that he work extra jobs, you just want more things, bigger house, or better toys (not judging) …then you guys might want to look at the budget of your household and maybe scale down a bit so he doesn't have to do it. Hey, I know it can be crazy money sometimes to work extra and it is hard to pass up! Just be realistic about the cost, and how you want your lives to be lived.

One thing Gilmartin recommends is any exercise right after shift for at least twenty minutes. Doing this will help lower these chemical reactions quicker. Because our heroes work this way consistently, it does affect them physically in many ways. I have heard from a few articles I have read that being a cop can lower your life expectancy by ten years. Having the knowledge of hyper-vigilance, and cumulative PTSD (Post Traumatic Stress Disorder) can change that statistic. Being aware of how this job will affect them just because they do this job can help deal with, and minimize the negative effects. It does not matter where they come from, or who they are, the body will react the same. Good news for you if you are a spouse of an officer!! It isn't you! Now I won't completely dismiss y'all cause I know some of you are off the chain with your hot mess!

I love you regardless, and coming alongside you and encouraging you to make some changes to start thriving in our life instead of trying to just survive it, is the reason for this book! Even in our mess we are not alone. When you start reaching out to other wives you will find out how similar your life and struggles are to theirs. Isolation is one of our biggest challenges. Don't think for a second that I have a stone to throw at anyone! I was the poster child for being a hot mess! Again, if you don't have this book, buy one for yourself and everyone in your family. Trust me on this, it can change everything in your relationship and how your friends and family relate to officers.

In 2007, we were blessed to partner with InFaith Missions that have been established for 200 years. Yes, that is correct 200 years (www.infaith.org). They are a missionary organization within the borders of the United States. When we spoke to them about our heart for our police community, they were amazed at what we shared with them. Chuck and I were not near staffed to become a 501c3 non-profit organization yet. We knew we needed stable, reliable, trustworthy people to cover us in the financial realm. They came alongside us and helped us learn many valuable things about outreach and ministry. At the writing of this book, we are grateful to say we are still in partnership with them and are blessed to have the guidance and support of Tim, Vivian, Joe, and all the staff of InFaith.

About that same time, we started doing law enforcement only events. We would rent out a movie theatre, or a bowling alley or something public but only police and their families was allowed in. It was a great thing to watch these guys relax a little with their families and have fun without always watching their back. We helped a local officer who had been injured in a crash while trying to get to a scene. We had a softball tournament and raised money for his family. That was really fun and such a blessing to watch our brothers support one another and all pitch in.

We continued to reach out, support, and equip officers and their families with free marriage coaching, and biblical counseling. In 2010 I became the first Police Chaplain for the Grandview Police Department in Grandview Texas. When I discovered a female could even be a chaplain I was floored? I knew this was where I belonged. The hand just seemed to fit in the glove perfectly. Three days after my first chaplain training I was dealing with a consistent back issue which has plagued me for 11 years. I had a temporary implant of a "Stimulator" device in my lower back which required I carry this little box around with me that were attached to the leads in my spine. I had just been home a day from the hospital when I got a call that one of our officers had been severely injured. He was Code 3 to assist a Deputy, and at the curve of a county road in the dark, he wrapped his unit around a tree. I went to the hospital immediately and stayed there to do whatever I could. It didn't matter about wires hanging out my shirt and carrying a stupid box, it was about him, and them.

This officer was indeed blessed to survive, however, some of his injuries forced him to retire from law enforcement. I learned so much form doing my best to serve and help him, I think about him even today, and always will.

In 2012, I started volunteering with the Burleson, Texas Police Department as Chaplain and continued my training with the International Conference of Police Chaplains (ICPC). Not long after, I was asked to be the Chaplain for a small town called Maypearl. It wasn't far from Grandview, so the triangle of agencies worked out well.

I was living the dream and Chuck was still working night shifts. The balance of ministry, shift work, and family was lots of work. Nothing about this life is easy. I began to see a more significant need for us, the spouses of officers. Most agencies didn't acknowledge spouse or even address the need for them to be aware of how the new recruit will change within a year. I began looking for something out there that we could partner with, we don't like reinventing the wheel. I found a ministry called "Wives On Duty" founded by Allison Uribe. What a beautiful find she was! We got together on the phone and discovered our passions were the same as our experiences! Man, I was so happy to find someone who "spoke my language!" Allison was in the midst of creating Wives On Duty chapters at that time, so we became her third one in Johnson County Texas. We had regular meetings, and our group was extraordinary. One thing to learn is though when you have a group of females, especially Type A which is usually the ones who marry cops, you will encounter drama. We really did well for three whole years which I think is a record!

Yet, someone was hurt, they became angry and then became hell-bent to destroy me and everything about me. This was in 2014, which became the year of trials, proving of my faith, and my calling. Due to highly charged emotional deception, one woman decided to try to remove me from all of my Chaplaincy positions by creating lies over an incident. She asked me to help one of our close friends who were in a dangerous and sensitive situation. I got counsel from my Pastor and my mentor on this situation to not only have accountability but to make sure I was prayed up and versed to give her what she needed. As always in these cases, you get permission from the one who shares this sensitive information with you to share with the person you will be helping.

Is it ok to tell them where I got this information? Confidentiality is paramount always when serving law enforcement, and really anyone for that matter! I was given permission to share where I received the intel on the situation. After our meeting together, our friend immediately went to the woman and asked if she has told me everything I was given permission to share. She denied ever even asking me to step in and that she told me anything. Betrayal is brutal. This was just the beginning of the assault. This woman called every agency I served with and even Allison with Wives On Duty to tell a different story and ask that I be removed from my office due to ethics violations. The end of the story here is that I chose to resign due to all of this swirling around. It really doesn't matter if I am telling the truth and she isn't. What matters is due to the drama around me I am no longer useful in my position because the guys don't want to get involved in all of that mess. If I cannot be a help and benefit to my officers, there is no need to be there. I include this in this book because it was indeed a pivoting point and a stone of remembrance for me in my walk with God.

No matter how hard you try to be what people need, you have no control how hurt people, will hurt people. As I look back I was working so hard to help the women I loved, I may have been too close. Mentoring and friendship have a delicate boundary line. For some, you can only be one or the other. A few months after all of this, on July 7, 2014, my eldest brother Reece Harper Jr, our beloved Spanky, took someone else's gun and shot himself in the head. This was the crushing blow to my family and me. He was only 52 years old. We all knew his wife was very emotionally and mentally abusive to him, but he just couldn't stay away from her. They married each other four times.

Who does that?! Someone who cannot make a way to escape from a toxic relationship. my mother knew he was depressed a bit, but the man hated guns. This one would be the first one he ever fired. None of our family could believe he would do that, and there were so many things that didn't pass the smell test. I will have questions concerning his death till I see Jesus face to face. That year was brutal, but it taught me so much about my understanding of this entire experience of life, and what matters. We get this vapor mist of time to discover ourselves, our world, and our purpose. Sometimes we get so focused on those things we lose sight of who designed us, created our world, and has a defined meaning for us. The temporary things in life can easily entangle us and shift our gaze from the eternal importance of what we are and what we were made for.

After the devastation of the summer of 2014, I took a leave of absence with Burleson PD, and Chuck and I decided we needed to let all that we had worked for with Bless The Badge the last 15 years, die. I knew in my heart that God wanted to completely restore and renew our hearts and minds for a season. This was one of the most difficult things we ever did. Closing websites, Facebook pages, bank accounts.... everything. We were willing to put all of our dreams, vision, and calling into the ground and walk away. We didn't know if God would ever resurrect it, or not. After all, it all belonged to Him, anyway.

Need some good news? Yeah!! Now you know the story doesn't end there! In 2016 God showed up in a very unusual way. We attend Victory Family Church in Burleson, (shout out to Pastor Mark Greenroy!) and I have a friend who was a new police wife visiting with us. Now they had been married a few years with a daughter, but he had just started in the police academy at the time. They began to experience some serious relationship challenges, and she began to talk to me about it. I won't go into much detail on this story, but if you ever get to one of our conferences, you will be amazed as they tell it. I won't steal their thunder here, but wow God shows Himself so strong sometimes! This couple finally met with us at a critical point, and it was an intense coaching session!

Chuck and I, by all accounts, could not see how this couple could survive the damage that had been done. But God. They went from arriving with attorneys chosen, a girlfriend waiting, and no plans to continue the marriage, to having an amazing and life-changing encounter with The One who defines and is Love. Only God can change a heart like that! This couple now serves on our Bless The Badge Team and received training to be marriage coaches!

So when you witness a miracle in front of you, you naturally are on a spiritual high. You can scale the mountains and move them by a word! I have tried drugs in the past, so I can tell you from my experience there ain't no high like a Holy Spirit High!! From experience with this couple, we started thinking about the need in our Blue Family with a staggering 75% divorce rate. Would God use us again to bring whatever we could to our precious families and help them learn how to navigate this crazy and unique life? It seemed so! A police wife contacted me right after this who had attended our first ever conference three years ago we did with Wives On Duty. She really wanted to do another one and really felt a strong call to reach out to her sisters in blue. So we prayed, and on 10-8-2016 we had our comeback conference in Fort Worth, Texas. It was so cool to have a comeback on 10-8 which is police code for "Back In Service!" This was what God was designing for us in this season. We gathered a group of wives with our same passion and formed a team.

At the writing of this book, we have done several conferences in Texas, and one in California! Next year we have planned one every month across the country until May of next year! What an incredible privilege it is to go and meet these heroes! The families of officers who are so courageous and sacrifice so much. If our communities had the slightest clue of what is behind every one of the street warriors that protect them, they would be amazed! Chuck and I had the retirement plan that most do. We want to move to Green Valley, Arizona and soak up the sun! Yet, we would not trade what we get the honor of doing for anything. We go and do what we can because we want to, not because we are paid to. I don't know how long we will hold up, you know Chuck is a bionic man now.

His shoulder is replaced, his hip is replaced, and he has a bum knee from his last call before he retired. I lost count of how many herniated discs I have, along with spinal stenosis, arthritis, scoliosis, neuropathy, fibromyalgia, a dissected Achilles Tendon, blah, blah, blah. One thing I know to be true! God's grace is sufficient, and when I am weak, He is strong. That, coupled with eternity in a new body living forever with my Creator and lover of my soul, is all I needed to know. As long as we are able, we will give all that we are to encourage, equip, and support our Blue families. We will strive to educate the community about The Line that protects them from chaos, and self-destruction. We have so many visions and dreams yet to happen! A Law Enforcement Retreat and Training Center that's FREE to all LE! Local programs in every county for LE family support, physically, emotionally, and financially. We will see what God will do!

"Blessed are those who hunger and thirst for righteousness, for they will be filled. Blessed are the merciful, for they will be shown mercy. Blessed are the pure in heart, for they will see God. Blessed are the peacemakers, for they will be called children of God. Blessed are those who are persecuted because of righteousness, for theirs is the kingdom of heaven." Matthew 5:6-10 NKJV

WHAT I WISH I KNEW THEN

Therefore, since we are surrounded by such a great cloud of witnesses, let us throw off everything that hinders and the sin that so easily entangles. And let us run with perseverance the race marked out for us, 2 fixing our eyes on Jesus, the pioneer and perfecter of faith.

— HEBREWS 12:1 NIV

Many times I have had police wives and even officers ask me the question "What do you know now that you wish you knew then"? That's a loaded question, right? There are seasons of this life where it would have been so much easier if I had some of the wisdom and knowledge I have now. Not that I have attained, mind you, I am still learning things every day! In the first season, I was new to the whole thing and no clue what police life was all about. I never met or even heard from anyone at the PD to help me in any way. In those days Chuck worked eight-hour shifts and changed shifts every thirty days. Oh, what a joyful time that was! I learned some critical skills then that helped me in the seasons to come. Flexibility. It really doesn't matter how well you schedule your life, your children's lives and activities... most of the time it isn't going to work. Late shifts, extra shifts, and additional jobs will see to that. So I learned to be flexible. Yes, it is good to have a schedule and a calendar, but it needs to be in pencil. I also learned that getting upset at him, for things at his job he cannot control didn't work well.

Believe me when I tell you your man wants to be at every celebration, every dinner, and every holiday. His job isn't one where he can just take off or call in sick. Know why? Because not only will it jeopardize his career, it leaves his shift mates hanging. That can be life-threatening when you are short a man, and the stuff hits the fan. Also, it leaves one less unit to answer calls and his guys suffer his loss as well as the community. I know, why should I care?! Because he chose this life and all of its sacrifices, and sweet darlin, you did too. You are his wife! Yeah I know, being a hero comes with a price. The first season I wish I had known the priceless value of having other wives around who lived what I did, felt like I did, and sacrificed as I did.

The next season is the one when the children arrive, and maybe you are working outside the home. Hey, believe me I know both worlds. We chose to give up a lot for me to stay home until our daughter started kindergarten. Then I went back to work. Staying home and working outside both have their unique challenges and not one outranks another to me. During this season the "single parent syndrome" tends to sneak in and it can really wreak havoc on a relationship. What I learned in this season was that my man needed to be needed. Now, everyone knows that women can pretty much take care of anything. We were designed to be helpmates. That means we are the definition of "what do you need? I got that." We can fix it, clean it, make it, dress it, cook it, calm it down, and leave it with a smile. It becomes easy to take care of everything since you are usually the only one there, or awake, to do it. We can't let that rob our men of their need to be our Man. Now don't get me wrong, he will not clean like you do, load the dishwasher like you do, or even change a lightbulb like you do. It's ok! You must allow him to do something around his domain! For goodness sake, if he does what you ask, never correct him.

The worst you can do, is to do it over again! I know you are cringing or laughing right now. I know, I did that! If you correct him or redo it, he will never do it again. Would you?! If he loads the dishwasher "wrong" according to you, what universal law has been broken?! In the scheme of the universe what damage has been done?! Just say, "Thank you Honey" and move on. There was a book I read about 10 years into our marriage. This was definitely something I wish I had from the beginning. It is "Love and Respect" by Dr. Emerson Eggerich. This teaching can change your life, it certainly changed our marriage! All these years I had been praying, fasting, throwing myself on the floor in little tantrums waiting for God to change this impossible man! As I read this book, I discovered something that never occurred to me. Maybe I had the issues? Shut The Front Door! Not me?! Well, yes my adorable precious wives it just could be you, just maybe. I had always been taught that you did not give a man respect until he earned it.

Society still teaches us that. But in relationship men and women are obviously different. For women, our DNA is love. We thrive on love, feeling loved, being loved. For men, their DNA is respect. They thrive on respect, feeling respected, being respected. One thing is clear, we must always separate behavior for the person. A person's behavior can be unlovable or disrespectful, but not the person. One thing you can always start with if your relationship is struggling in this is; He is a man made in the image of God, and he is your man. That alone is enough to give the man the respect he deserves. What you will find is that once you begin to see ways you can show him respect, and even get real crazy and tell him you respect him, he will change! I fought and nagged him to help me do things around the house all the time. Once I began to change my behavior toward him, and began asking, not demanding and criticizing, and always demonstrated to him respect, I no longer had to ask. That man took out the trash All. By. Himself! It was a miracle! He wanted to do the things I asked him to do, and he actually did more things I didn't even ask! If you were looking for the "magic" to motivate your man, I could testify that genuinely learning to respect him, and show it is something that works!

As our daughter grew our lives shifted with high school insane schedules, and I was now working full time and traveling with my job as a Regional Manager in merchandising. This season of life comes with a new set of challenges and what I wish someone would have told me then is to be intentional about our marriage. Even for women who do not have full time jobs, a schedule of shift work, kid's schedules, family activities are just as busy as when you hold down a job outside the home. It is easy for you both to start living your own lives. He is consumed with all that pertains to his work plus extra jobs they usually work, and you mostly being a single parent due to that.

If you do not become intentional about spending time with each other, investing in your relationship, you will one day find you don't even know who is other is and why you should even be married. This task will not be easy, and it will take effort on both parts to make this happen. Everything around you will always be competing for your time. The best thing you can ever do for your children is to demonstrate to them how much you put each other first. It really is ok to put them before your children. When children are a higher priority than each other, it will not end well, and your children will be imbalanced in all of their future relationships. During those days I have to admit, my daughter and my job seemed to be more of a priority than my husband. There were many things I wish I would have done differently, and I know nothing now can change the past. I am so grateful we were able to discuss our failures and love each other through them. Grace and forgiveness is free, bitterness and judgement are costly and can be fatal.

As far as relationship building goes I guess the last thing I wish I knew then was our Love Languages. Dr. Gary Smalley wrote the book, *The 5 Love Languages* that was to us another game changer. There are 5 basic love languages and you usually have one dominant one. They are Acts of Service, Words Of Affirmation, Physical Touch, Gifts, and Quality Time. Not only is it beneficial to know what you and your mate's love language is, but your children, family, and friends. When you understand how you perceive love, and how your mate perceives it you can then learn how to speak it. This changed our relationship drastically because I was not raised in a family that was very physically affectionate. We didn't hug each other or touch each other much. Chuck, my husband happened to speak Physical Touch as his primary love language.

So for me, I had to become intentional on learning how to speak that to him. Of course my first thought was, Great, now I gotta have sex every day! (And all the men said Hail Yeah!), but actually you have to ask what that looks like for them. For him, it was just that I touch or scratch his back when I am around him, or hug him, or sit close to him. His second high ranked language was Quality Time. Again, what does that look like to him? I don't want to spend every waking minute with him staring at his handsome face if that doesn't do it for him. As with most guys, he just wanted me to be "present" with him.

To watch TV with him, work on a project with him, or drive around and do something he likes. Now during these time, we may not get into much conversation, so we ladies will just have to chew our tongues if need be. This is his way of receiving love, not ours. Guys can spend a whole day together working on something and maybe say two words between them. They will feel satisfied that they spent some great time together and it was even "fun"! Now we know that does not come close to our definition of fun and a good time spent with someone if there is no conversation happening! We have to understand and accept our differences as male and female. If we both talked no one would listen, if we both just listened no talking would happen. Balance my beloved, balance.

I learned to sit with him, and I learned to reach out and touch him, and hug him even when I didn't particularly need either of those behaviors to feel loved. But I wanted to love him how he wanted to be loved, so I learned. What is my love language you ask? Oh, thanks for asking. Mine is Acts Of Service. Yeah, baby, you can send me flowers and hold my hand, but if you wash the dishes and vacuum, I am tuned up and ready to go! Since I am disabled with back and nerve disorders it prevents me from keeping my house, and doing other things I used to do. I am even more appreciative when anyone helps me with things I can no longer do myself. I recommend you get the book so you read about your particular language.

Just taking the test will tell you what you are, but it won't explain them for you. It is really important how your mate can speak them for you, and what theirs looks like to them. One last thing about that. You will also discover that you can deeply hurt one another by behavior that directly speaks their language as well. For example if my husband's language is Quality Time, and every time we are together someone else is involved, or I am on my phone... that will affect him deeply because that's how he receives love from me. Get that? Or if your language is Words Of Affirmation, and he never tells you how good you are, how well you do things, or listens and affirms your feelings? That cuts deeper than if you didn't get to spend time together.

Now that we finally have reached the pinnacle, the career finish line it seems surreal. Retiring is what we all pray for. To live long enough to make it, and to make it intact with each other. It was hard to know what to do the first year. We spent more time together in the first year than we all the last 27, awake! I was so happy to finally be there and to still love each other. One thing I did not expect was to feel guilty. The last 5-8 years of his career we witnessed the extreme shift in society towards our heroes and our police community. I had always shared in those struggles with my blue family, and now it felt like I was leaving them behind. I literally felt bad for us retiring! Isn't that strange?

Police life was all either of us knew as a couple. We made plans as everyone does of that house in Tucson, fishing every day, and traveling. Yet, we knew we just couldn't walk away. Our hearts had been seared into Blue. God's call is without repentance and an expiration date this side of Heaven it seems. We discovered that our retirement dream was looking a bit different than we planned. It wasn't to walk away from The Line after pouring our lives, our hearts, and our souls in it. It was to discover that all we poured into it, had filled us to overflowing. It was now time to stand up, turn around, and start pouring back into that courageous Blue Line, all that had been poured into us.

"Therefore, since we are surrounded by such a great cloud of witnesses, let us throw off everything that hinders and the sin that so easily entangles. And let us run with perseverance the race marked out for us, 2 fixing our eyes on Jesus, the pioneer and perfecter of faith." Hebrews 12:1 NIV

EPILOGUE

What a journey writing this first book has been. It has been a work in progress for years and such a rollercoaster. God has been writing my story and I knew someday I would put into print the amazing landscape my life has been. I don't know if you are in the law enforcement life, or if you are just curious about what it looks like. To those of you not in the police life reading my story, I hope this has been eye opening for you.

There are so many in society that do not understand what it means to wear that uniform, and how it affects their entire family. Hopefully this book has encouraged you to share with others the truths you learned here that you can take to your sphere of influence and start some conversations. For my blue family, know that I love you even though I haven't met you. My heart is forever entwined with those who sacrifice so much in life in our little subcultures within our society.

There are so many stories to write and so much experience to share I knew I couldn't get it all in one book. In 2018 we will be doing conferences all over the U.S. and I sure hope to meet some of you face to face! Whatever we have planned with its location will be on our website www.blessthebadge.com.

I am giving you my email to hear your feedback. I want to know if anything was beneficial, and may be what you would like to hear more about.

Email me at chaplainlerner@gmail.com.

Between Chuck and I, there are 30 years of writing, encouraging, and equipping we are dedicated to providing.

If your city, or county would like to have a workshop done at your agency, or have a conference done in your area please contact us. We do not charge any fees for speaking anywhere, it's our privilege. We work hard to never have an event we have to charge for either.

So far, we haven't, and we pray for sponsors that want to help our police communities in supporting us in keeping them free. Chuck and I do not receive any salary or income from conferences, workshops, or any speaking engagements. Any money received goes into our account with InFaith as missionaries to Law Enforcement and every penny is used for Bless The Badge Ministries. If you or anyone you know is interested in supporting us on a regular basis we would be honored! You can find us on the www.infaith.org site and set up regular or one-time support and receive the benefit of a tax-deductible receipt.

Yeah, I know, I had to throw all that in before I closed it out. I ain't too proud to ask for support of what I know changes lives, and has even saved them. Thank you for purchasing this book, and reading my story. Until, next time watch your sister's six, and love that hero the best you know how. In our reality of having one day at a time, make them count. For my "civilian" friends, thank you for all of your support and prayers for law enforcement. I am truly grateful.

Chaplain Lisa Harper Lerner

Bless The Badge Ministries

ABOUT THE AUTHOR

Chaplain Lisa Lerner is a veteran Police Wife being married to her husband Chuck for 28 years. He retired as a police officer in 2016 after 30 years of service beginning in El Paso, Texas and retiring from Cleburne, Texas. The Lerner's have a beautiful 26 year old daughter who is a Southwestern Assemblies of God University graduate and served with the Forest Hill Police Department as a dispatcher.

Chaplain Lisa Lerner is an ordained minister and has served in law enforcement ministry with Chuck since 1990. Lisa served as Chaplain with the Grandview, Texas Police Department as their first agency Police Chaplain. She currently serves Burleson, Texas Police Department. She continued her education and obtained her Biblical Counseling Certification in 2014. She pursued studies in Critical Incident Stress Management (CISM) and serves as

Chaplain for the Johnson County CISM Team.

Together, Lisa and Chuck founded "Bless The Badge Ministries" in 2002.

Their heart and passion for the law enforcement community has continued past retirement. They currently provide free marriage coaching, biblical counseling, and are speakers at Bless The Badge Conferences and Workshops nationwide.

For More Information:
www.blessthebadge.com
chaplainlerner@gmail.com

www.ingramcontent.com/pod-product-compliance
Lightning Source LLC
Chambersburg PA
CBHW070627300426
44113CB00010B/1689